Zebras

Zebras

Jenny Markert

THE CHILD'S WORLD®, INC.

Published in the United States of America by The Child's World®, Inc.
PO Box 326
Chanhassen, MN 55317-0326
800-599-READ
www.childsworld.com

Product Manager Mary Berendes
Editor Katherine Stevenson
Designer Mary Berendes
Contributor Bob Temple

Photo Credits
© Adam Jones, The National Audubon Society Collection/Photo Researchers: 13
© 2001 Art Wolfe/Stone: 24
© 1993 Craig Brandt: 30
© 1995 Craig Brandt: 19
© 1997 Craig Brandt: cover
© Dave Hamman/ABPL, The National Audubon Society Collection/Photo Researchers: 20
© Joe McDonald/www.hoothollow.com: 9
© 1998 Kevin Schafer: 15, 26
© 2001 Manoj Shah/Stone: 10
© 1995 Robin Brandt: 16
© 1997 Robin Brandt: 2, 23
© 1992 Stan Osolinski/Dembinsky Photo Assoc. Inc.: 6, 29

Library of Congress Cataloging-in-Publication Data
Markert, Jenny.
Zebras / by Jenny Markert.
p. cm.
Includes index.
ISBN 1-56766-883-6 (library bound : alk. paper)
1. Zebras—Juvenile literature. [1. Zebras.] I. Title.
QL737.U62 M37 2001
599.665'7—dc21
00-010782

On the cover...

Front cover: This Burchell's zebra lives in Hluhluwe National Park in South Africa.
Page 2: This Burchell's zebra has found a shady spot to rest on a hot afternoon.

Table of Contents

The hot afternoon sun beats down on the African plain. In the distance a herd of animals stands grazing on the grass. They look a lot like horses, but they're not black or brown or white like regular horses. Instead, they have bold black and white stripes all over their bodies. What are these colorful animals? They're zebras!

⇐ These Cape mountain zebras live in a national park in South Africa.

What Are Zebras?

Zebras are members of the horse family. Donkeys and mules are also zebra relatives. All of these animals have long bodies with four strong legs. Their feet have hard, sturdy hooves that help the animals run fast and protect themselves. But zebras have one thing that their horse relatives don't—stripes. Most zebras are covered with black and white stripes, and some have brown stripes, too.

There are three main groups of zebras. Each group looks slightly different. *Burchell's zebras* (also called *plains zebras*) have wide stripes that go all the way under their belly. *Grevy's zebras* have a white belly, narrow stripes, and large, round ears. *Mountain zebras* have a white belly and a square flap of skin on their throat.

This Burchell's zebra is eating with its herd in Kenya. ⇒

Zebras live on the grassy plains of Africa. They share the grasslands with giraffes, wildebeests, and many other plant-eating animals. Like the other animals, zebras are hunted by meat-eating animals called **predators** that roam the plains. The biggest predator of zebras is the lion.

← Here a lioness is hunting a small herd of zebras in Kenya.

Why Do Zebras Have Stripes?

Many animals are colored to blend in with their surroundings. This coloring helps them hide from enemies or sneak up on their meals. Coloring or markings that help an animal hide are called **camouflage.** A zebra's stripes can work as camouflage to hide the animal in tall grass.

No two zebras have the same stripes. In fact, a zebra's stripes are a lot like your fingerprints! To tell two zebras apart, you need to look closely—especially at their shoulders. There the stripes are the most different from zebra to zebra.

The stripes of this Burchell's zebra make the shape ⇒ of its body harder to see in the tall grass.

Away from tall grass, the zebra's stripes seem all too easy to see. But they do blend in with the waves of heat that rise above the plains. Scientists also think the stripes might help the animal stay comfortable in changing weather. The white stripes reflect the sun's heat, while the black stripes soak it up.

Another special thing about a zebra's stripes is that they confuse enemies. When zebras stand together, all of their stripes blend into one another. It's much harder for a predator to pick out just one animal to attack.

It's hard to pick out just one animal ⇒
in this herd of Burchell's zebras.

Besides hiding, zebras have other ways of protecting themselves from lions. Like horses, zebras have strong, muscular legs. Healthy zebras can run faster and farther than lions—up to 40 miles an hour. A zebra uses its hard hooves to kick an enemy that comes too close.

⟸ You can see the hooves of this Grevy's zebra as it runs in Kenya.

Zebras also protect themselves by living in large groups called **herds.** To be safe, all the zebras in the herd are always alert. They use their keen eyesight and hearing to detect enemies. The more eyes that can watch for danger, the better!

If a zebra senses danger, it makes quick barking noises. Then the whole herd darts off in all directions. If one of the zebras waits even a second, the enemy might be upon it. Usually, the enemy chases the easiest animals to catch—the old or the weak.

This herd of Grant's zebras (a type of plains zebra) is ⇒ staying safe by mixing in with a herd of wildebeests. This way, there are even more eyes to look for danger.

Even at night, zebras must be on the lookout for enemies. Zebra herds spend the night in open spaces where they can see approaching lions. Most zebras sleep lying down, but the leader of the herd sleeps standing up. The leader is a male, called a **stallion.** He is usually the strongest member of the herd. He watches over and protects the other zebras.

⇐ This herd of Burchell's zebras was just getting ready to settle down for the night. The stallion sensed danger, and they are following him to safety.

What Do Zebras Eat?

Besides providing safety, the open plains have grass, roots, and leafy plants zebras like to eat. During the rainy season, the herds can find water, too. Water holes are full, and zebras usually stay nearby.

In the dry season, water is harder to find. Zebras might have to travel long distances to find enough to drink. They travel to large lakes or rivers where they can usually find water.

These Burchell's zebras are getting a drink ⇒ in a national park in South Africa.

Many African animals flock to the dry-season water holes. Zebras are likely to run into other zebra herds. When they do, the stallions greet each another by sniffing and touching noses. Sometimes they flash their front teeth, each animal warning the other to stay away. If neither stallion backs down, the two zebras fight. They knock into each other, kick, and bite. The winner of the battle chases the other zebra away.

⇐ Here you can see two Grevy's zebra stallions fighting for control of a herd.

Are Zebras in Danger?

In the wild, zebras live to be about 20 years old. Each year, however, fewer and fewer zebras roam the African plains. Some zebras are killed by hunters who want to own the animal's flashy coat. Zebras must compete with other animals (including cattle raised by people) for food and water. In addition, people are moving into the open grasslands, so the plains become smaller every year. If the land is not preserved, many of the animals that live there could become **extinct,** or die out.

Grevy's zebras like this one have dangerously low numbers. ⇒

The zebra's brilliant colors are mysterious and striking. Are zebras black with white stripes, or are they just the opposite? Scientists think they are white with black stripes. What do you think?

Glossary

camouflage (KAM-oo-flahj)
Camouflage is coloring or special markings that make an animal look like the objects around it. A zebra's stripes act as camouflage, hiding the zebra in tall grass.

colts (KOLTS)
Young male horses are called colts. The same name is used for young male zebras.

extinct (ex-TINKT)
When a kind of animal completely dies out, it is said to become extinct. Without enough living space, zebras could one day become extinct.

fillies (FILL-eez)
Young female horses are called fillies. Young female zebras are called fillies, too.

foal (FOLE)
A very young baby horse is called a foal. The same word is also used for baby zebras.

herds (HERDZ)
Herds are groups of animals that live together. Zebras live in herds.

mare (MEHR)
A mare is a female horse or zebra. Zebra mares give birth to a single baby at a time.

predators (PREH-deh-terz)
Predators are animals that hunt and eat other animals. Lions are predators that often hunt zebras.

stallion (STAL-yun)
Male zebras are called stallions. The leader of a zebra herd is a stallion.

Web Sites

http://www.imh.org/imh/bw/zebra.html

http://www.awf.org/animals/zebra.html

http://www.panda.org/kids/wildlife/mnzebra.htm

Index